# SQUANTO
# and the first
# THANKSGIVING

# SQUANTO
# and the first
# THANKSGIVING

by JOYCE K. KESSEL
pictures by LISA DONZE

Carolrhoda Books ✦ Minneapolis

*This book is available in two editions:*
Library binding by Carolrhoda Books, Inc.
Soft cover by First Avenue Editions
241 First Avenue North
Minneapolis, Minnesota 55401

LIBRARY OF CONGRESS CATALOGING-IN-PUBLICATION DATA

Kessel, Joyce
  Squanto and the first Thanksgiving.

  (A Carolrhoda on my own book)
  Summary: Describes how the Indian Squanto, an
English-speaking Christian and former slave, whose
village had been wiped out by smallpox, taught the
Pilgrims the skills they needed to survive the harsh
Massachusetts winter.
  1. Thanksgiving Day—Juvenile literature. 2. Squanto
—Juvenile literature. [1. Squanto. 2. Wampanoag
Indians—Biography. 3. Indians of North America—
Massachusetts—Biography. 4. Pilgrims (New Plymouth
Colony) 5. Thanksgiving Day] I. Donze, Lisa, ill.
II. Title. III. Series.
GT4975.K47   1983     970.004'97 [92]     82-10313
ISBN 0-87614-199-8(lib bdg.)
ISBN 0-87614-452-0 (pbk.)

5  6  7  8  9  10  88  87  86

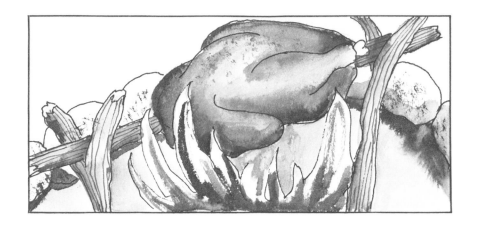

for Ric, Allison, and Sean
—J.K.K.

for my mother and father
—L.D.

For thousands of years,
people all over the world
have set aside special days
for giving thanks.
People in the U.S. and Canada
have celebrated Thanksgiving
for over 350 years.
How did Thanksgiving start?
Most of us think right away
of the Pilgrims,
but the story really begins with
a Patuxet Indian named Squanto.
Without Squanto, the Pilgrims
would never have celebrated
that first Thanksgiving.

The Patuxet tribe lived near
the place we now call
Plymouth, Massachusetts.
There they grew corn
and hunted wild animals.
They were friendly and peaceful.

Then, in the early 1600s,

an English ship came to Plymouth.

These Englishmen were explorers.

They were looking for riches.

They hoped to find gold or silver,

but all they found

was corn and Indians.

The Englishmen had never seen corn.

They didn't know what to do with it.

But they thought they knew

what to do with Indians.

They would sell them as slaves!

So the Englishmen captured
a few Patuxet braves.
They took the Patuxets to England
and sold them.
Squanto was one of those Patuxets.

When he got to England,

he was sold as a slave.

He had to learn

how to speak English,

and he had to work very hard.

Squanto was used to hard work.

The Plymouth winters

were long and cold.

Sometimes Squanto had been hungry

all winter long.

But the rest of the year

had brought riches.

The woods of his home

were full of berries

and wild animals.

And even when he had been hungry,

he had been free.

Squanto longed for his home.
He dreamed of his people
and of his wild, free land.
His master could see
that Squanto was not happy.
He felt sorry for his slave.
Finally he set Squanto free.
In 1614 Captain John Smith
sailed for the New World.
Squanto went with him!
He returned at last to his tribe.
But not for long!

Captain Smith sailed back to England,
but he left one of his ships behind.
The captain of that ship
was named Thomas Hunt.
Hunt traded with the Patuxets.
He filled his ship
with fish and animal furs.
But Hunt was greedy.
He wanted to make more money
than the fish and furs would bring.
So he also filled part of his ship
with Patuxet braves.
Squanto was captured again!
After only a few weeks at home,
he was sailing back across the ocean.

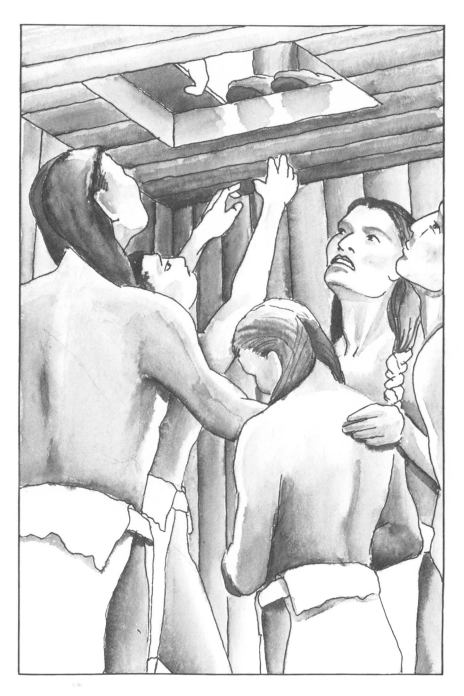

Hunt knew that Captain Smith
would be angry with him
for capturing the Patuxets.
So Hunt sold the Patuxets
in Spain instead of England.

Squanto's new masters
were Catholic monks.
They taught him the Christian faith.
They were kind to him,
but, of course,
Squanto was sadder than ever.
All he wanted was his freedom.
At last the monks took pity on him.
They helped him get to England.

From England Squanto was able
to find a ship going to America.
He was on his way home again!
But what great sadness
he found when he arrived.
Squanto could not believe his eyes!
All the Patuxets were dead!
He wandered through empty villages.
All he found were crumbling huts.
The once-green cornfields
lay black and dead.
All the people were gone.
Squanto was the only living Patuxet!

What had happened?

A neighboring tribe told him.

His people had all been killed

by the "white man's plague."

The ships from England

had brought smallpox germs.

Smallpox was a new disease

to the Patuxets,

so they died quickly from it.

After all those years

of longing for his home,

Squanto found he had no home.

He moved in

with a neighboring tribe.

Squanto had been back for one year
when the Pilgrims landed
at Plymouth, Massachusetts.
That was on December 21, 1620.
The Pilgrims were English.
They had left England
to look for a new home
where people would let them
worship God the way they chose.
They were lucky to land at Plymouth.
The Patuxets were all dead,
and the other Indians
were afraid of smallpox.
So there were no angry Indians
ready to fight for their land.

The Indians just watched
from a distance.

The Pilgrims had been townspeople.
They did not know how to plant.

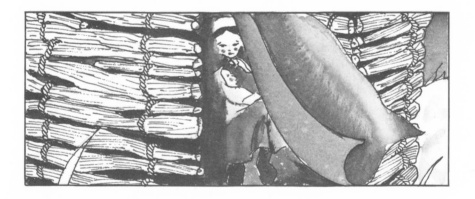

They did not know how to build.
They made cold, little houses
out of mud, clay, and sticks.

They were not used to the cold,
and they did not have much to eat.
During their first terrible winter,
half of the Pilgrims died.
By the spring of 1621,
there were only 55 of them left.

That was when Squanto
decided to help them.
Squanto knew that the Pilgrims
were Christians.
None of the other Indians
were Christians,
but when Squanto had lived in Spain,
he had become a Christian.
Also, Squanto knew
how to speak English.
So in 1621
he went to visit the Pilgrims.
After his first visit,
he never left them.

Squanto taught the Pilgrims
how to find animals
to shoot for meat.
He showed them
how to build warm houses.
He helped them make friends
with the neighboring Indians.
He explained how to plant.
He told them to watch
the leaves on the trees.
When they were as big
as squirrels' ears,
the corn should be planted.
He taught the Pilgrim women
how to cook the corn.

Squanto and the Pilgrims
worked very hard
all spring and summer,
and in the fall
the harvest was a good one.
Because of Squanto's help,
the Pilgrims would have warm homes
and plenty to eat through the winter.

The Pilgrims wanted to celebrate.

They wanted to give thanks.

They decided to have a feast.

They sent Squanto to invite

an Indian chief named Massasoit

to their dinner.

They thought that Massasoit

might bring a few braves too.

Thanksgiving feasts
were not new to the Indians.
Theirs was called
the "Green Corn Dance,"
and it was a huge feast,
so Massasoit brought 90 braves
to the Pilgrims' "Green Corn Dance!"
The Pilgrims were very surprised,
but they tried not to show it.
There were 55 Pilgrims
and 92 Indians.
That made 147 people!
The Pilgrims were not sure
they had enough food for everyone.
They had better get busy!

For three days
the women did nothing but cook.

When the day for the feast arrived,
everything was ready.

What a feast it was!

The Indians had brought five deer.

The women made these into stew.

They roasted turkeys,

geese, and ducks.

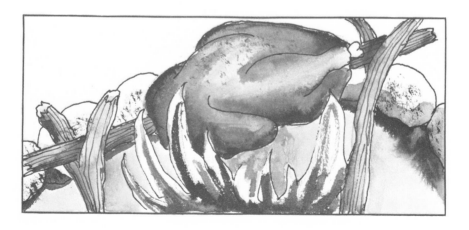

They cooked lobsters, eels,
clams, oysters, and fish.
They made biscuits and bread.
They roasted corn for "hoe cakes."

They boiled corn with molasses
to make "Indian pudding."
There was plenty of dried fruit
for everyone.

There may even have been
popcorn balls,
since they were invented
by the Indians in that area.

Usually the Pilgrims thought
that games were a waste of time,
but on this day they gave in.
Red and white men held contests.
They leaped and jumped and raced.

Everyone showed off.
The Pilgrim men marched,
the Indians shot arrows,
and, of course, people ate
until they could hardly move.

What a joyous day
that first Thanksgiving was.
The Pilgrims had new, warm homes.
They had new friends
and plenty of food.
They knew they would be able
to live through the next winter.
And none of it would have happened
without a Patuxet Indian
named Squanto.

# Afterword

Things did not turn out to be as easy as they looked on that first Thanksgiving. The winter that followed was even worse than the first for the Pilgrims. Then three more ships sailed into Plymouth. They brought hundreds of people, but no food. The crop in 1622 was not a good one, so there was no Thanksgiving that year. Thanksgiving was celebrated again in 1623, but it was celebrated in July to give thanks for rain.

For years there was no official day for Thanksgiving. People celebrated it whenever they felt like it. Then in 1864 President Lincoln named the last Thursday in November as the official U.S. Thanksgiving. In 1939 President Roosevelt changed it to the third Thursday. Then in 1941 it was changed back again.

Today people in the United States celebrate Thanksgiving on the last Thursday of November. People in Canada celebrate it on the second Monday in October.